Girl in the
Goldfish Bowl

Girl in the Goldfish Bowl

Morris Panych

Talonbooks
2003

Talonbooks
P.O. Box 2076, Vancouver, British Columbia, Canada V6B 3S3
www.talonbooks.com

Typeset in New Baskerville and printed and bound in Canada.

Second Printing: September 2005

National Library of Canada Cataloguing in Publication Data
Panych, Morris
  Girl in the goldfish bowl / Morris Panych

A play.
ISBN 0-88922-481-1

I. Title.
PS8581.A65G57 2003   C812'.54   C2003-910972-0

The publisher gratefully acknowledges the financial support of the Canada Council for the Arts; the Government of Canada through the Book Publishing Industry Development Program; and the Province of British Columbia through the British Columbia Arts Council for our publishing activities.

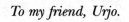

To my friend, Urjo.

Girl in the Goldfish Bowl premiered at the Arts Club Theatre Company in Vancouver in March, 2002 with the following cast and crew:

MR. LAWRENCE . . . . Zachary Ansley
SYLVIA . . . . Jennifer Clement
IRIS . . . . Leslie Jones
OWEN . . . . Tom Scholte
ROSE . . . . Meredith Bain Woodward
Directed by Patrick McDonald
Set Design: Ken MacDonald
Lighting Design: Marsha Sibthorpe
Costume Design: Nancy Bryant
Sound Design: John McCulloch
Stage Manager: Caryn Fehr

Girl in the Goldfish Bowl subsequently opened at the Tarragon Theatre in Toronto in September, 2002 with the following cast and crew:

MR. LAWRENCE . . . . Richard Zeppieri
SYLVIA . . . . Brenda Robins
IRIS . . . . Kristina Nicoll
OWEN . . . . John Jarvis
ROSE . . . . Tanja Jacobs
Directed by Morris Panych
Set Design: Ken MacDonald
Lighting Design: John Thompson
Costume Design: Ken MacDonald
Sound Design: Derek Bruce
Stage Manager: Tanya Greve

Kristina Nicoll as IRIS, and Richard Zeppieri as MR. LAWRENCE, in *Girl in the Goldfish Bowl*, by Morris Panych, at the Tarragon Theatre, Toronto, September–October 2002.

Photos by Cylla von Tiedemann.

Act One

Blackout. A plunge into water. Bubbles. Lights up on IRIS, a precocious girl of ten, in the front room of an old house, whose walls are dipped in verdigris, like a place submerged underwater at high tide. IRIS, wearing swimming goggles, is practicing her backstroke as her parents try to ignore her.

IRIS

These are the last few days of my childhood.

SYLVIA

(*Reading*) Iris.

OWEN

(*Drawing*) Please.

IRIS

It was pleasant enough while it lasted. A simple life of hollyhocks and squished beetles and jam.

She swims around the room.

My parents won't notice, of course. They're preoccupied with other things

OWEN

(*Lost in his drawing*) Don't say preoccupied; you're not old enough.

IRIS

My mother says you know when you've grown up.

Head in her mother's lap.

It's the moment you stop being happy, and start remembering when you used to be.

She sighs.

SYLVIA

Get—off.

The music continues, and lights change slowly in this house constructed of her imagination and memory. There is fog inside and out. As she speaks, the parents exit into their own worlds; SYLVIA to the kitchen, OWEN to the cellar.

I live in a country where nothing happens. In a town where nothing happens. In a house, where nothing much has ever really happened. Until now. October. It's just before my eleventh birthday. There's a fog prowling our street. Hiding in ditches. Peering through windows. I've gone for a walk along the water. Balancing a copy of *The Catholic Sunday Missal* on my head, introduction by Bishop Sheen, I step carefully over the rocks, one foot gracefully in front of the other. Poise is essential in times such as this. I am practicing to be a member of the Royal Family. Further up there are fires, and smelt fishermen are casting their nets, and further still the metal boats slapping against the dock, but here everything is quiet. I begin the solemn service. The moon puts in a brief appearance. And I know there are crabs hiding under the rocks, but otherwise, I am alone. Here beneath this arbutus tree, I pray for his little soul. If you expect your goldfish to ever get to heaven, you probably shouldn't whoosh him down the toilet. But my mother did, anyway. So I'm burying this frozen fish stick in his honour.

She crosses herself.

How will the world survive without Amahl, I wonder. I don't believe it will. This morning, there was an air-raid siren at school, and immediately I knew what had happened. Poor little Amahl. All night, last night, I watched him, trying so valiantly to upright himself in the bowl. One eye looking helplessly upward. Mother watched him, too. My father watched her. And we all fell together into a deep, deep well of sadness. So when I heard the siren this morning, I realized. He held the whole world together.

MISS ROSE

(*Appearing in isolation*) And how exactly did he do that?

IRIS

Don't ask me. It's a complete mystery. You just have to believe it.

MISS ROSE

Is that right?

The light opens and in the background, MISS ROSE prepares to go out.

IRIS

And while everyone scrambled to get under their desks—it was only a drill—I sat upright and said an act of Contrition on behalf of Amahl, who, according to Sister Anamelda, will have to spend an undisclosed amount of time in limbo. A place for the unbaptised, not far from heaven, which for some inexplicable reason is named after a popular party dance. Tonight, the "The Lonely Bull" by Herb Alpert, crackles over the radio as we wait for news. The whole world, now, is holding it's breath. Not only are there Russian missiles in Cuba. Elizabeth Taylor is still with Eddie Fisher. Poor Debbie Reynolds.

MISS ROSE

If anybody needs me, I'll be at the legion.

IRIS

There's going to be an atomic war, in case you're interested. Oh, by the way. My fish died. I hope that makes you happy.

MISS ROSE

Never become too emotionally attached to anything that flushes down the toilet—dearie.

She exits.

IRIS

Miss Rose works at the cannery. People who gut fish all day are very cynical. My mother, meanwhile, is upstairs with her feet propped on a pillow and a cold washcloth on her

1962

14

forehead. My father waits beside her, saying nothing. Listening to her every breath. Ordinarily, he sits and doodles at his drafting table all day, and dreams about Paris. He wants to stand under the Arc de Triomphe, gazing down the Champs d'Elysee all the way to the Louvre. Apparently, it's a moment of sublime geometry.

OWEN appears with a map of Paris; he sighs.

IRIS

See? Or to look down any one of the other avenues, leading off, at thirty perfect degrees, in twelve equal directions. Perhaps, in this way, my father will find what's been missing inside of him since before I was even born. Don't ask me what it is. I'm not a psychiatrist.

OWEN enters with a hot water bottle.

IRIS

I was an existentialist for a while, but nobody at school even knew what that was.

OWEN

I thought people your age ran away from home.

IRIS

I can't. I have a vocation.

OWEN

A what?

IRIS

Someone has to save this family.

OWEN

Have been talking to those nuns, again?

IRIS

I go to a Catholic school, for your information.

OWEN

Whose idea was that?

IRIS

Yours.

OWEN

Really?

> *OWEN exits. IRIS is alone. She digs out a secret box of old of photos.*

IRIS

My mother's only true love was an Australian motorcyclist named Arnie, who was killed in France, in the line of duty, January 17th, 1944. So every year, on the 17th day of January, my mother goes down at twilight, and sits at the end of the pier, looking south-east. She's never really loved my father.

> *SYLVIA appears in a wedding veil, sighs.*

IRIS

But when he came back from the war in a stretcher, she decided to marry him anyway.

> *SYLVIA evaporates.*

Now and again we take in boarders because my father can't really work. Once, a Chinese man lived with us who was a Buddhist. Every day he scaled salmon in twelve hour shifts, for two whole years, so he could bring his wife from China. But she never came. And so, one day, he left the house at eleven p.m., and he wandered down to the arbutus tree and he sat down and just died. It was a medical mystery. We went to his funeral and lit firecrackers. After, my father got me a goldfish, which I named Amahl because that's where we bought him. Every evening, my mother and my father would sit, and read, sometimes for hours and hours, and every once in a while, my mother would look up at Amahl, turning his circles, and my father would look over at her, and they would both take a deep breath, as if they were coming up for air. From where I sat, on the other side of the bowl, it seemed like life might just go on like this forever. Swimmingly. And that's how things were on our street until this morning. On October the twenty-second, in the Year of our Lord nineteen hundred and sixty-two, Amahl passed away quietly. This afternoon, as the President of the United States was delivering his ultimatum to the Russians, my mother decided to leave my father forever. She packed her bags and she said goodbye, but as she was leaving she stumbled and fell and broke her wrist. The doctor came and he said it wasn't serious, but he doesn't know the whole story. Now my father sits beside her bed, never once closing his eyes, never sleeping, but dreaming about Paris all the same. Because one day, he hopes to take my mother there. And on that day, he thinks she will finally love him. Owing to the alignment of the streets. Would you like a cocktail?

reincarnation
of the goldfish

LAWRENCE

What have you got?

MR. LAWRENCE appears out of nowhere.

IRIS

Crème de menthe. It's quite lovely. Or there's Chartreuse.

LAWRENCE

Do you have—ginger ale? I don't mean ginger ale. I mean—water?

IRIS

Are you afraid of communists?

LAWRENCE

Just—dogs. And—what?

Beat.

1st Beat

IRIS

We don't normally get overnight visitors at this time of year.

Beat.

IRIS

Are you a poet by any chance?

LAWRENCE

Why?

IRIS

You just seem that way.

LAWRENCE

Yeah?

IRIS

If there's an atomic war, everybody will have to eat canned spaghetti for a whole month. Imagine. Mr. DaSilva says the world is divided, now, because everyone within themselves is divided. But he's bound to say that sort of thing because he's Portuguese. Besides, he's blind, so it's allowed. It's like when an Italian kisses your hand. If an ordinary person did that, you'd just think it was creepy. You're very handsome, you know. But in an unconventional way.

> *Looking at him more closely.*

You don't really have any ear lobes to speak of.

LAWRENCE
> No?

IRIS
> I can make you a Manhattan if you like.

LAWRENCE
> Did you say how, how old you were?

IRIS
> Almost eleven. Mr. DaSilva says I have a very old soul, though. Do you believe in reincarnation, by the way?

> Miss Rose thinks that a human being is the lowest thing you can become. She's our one and only boarder at the moment. She works at the cannery, and she keeps the temperature in her room about a million degrees. I hate to say it, but she smells just a little like fresh halibut. Even though she has about six lavender baths a day. She soaks forever and she never, ever drains the tub. This is my father's drafting table. Do you like it? It's made completely out of oak.

Iris is divided Young/old. internal conflict

19

LAWRENCE

Congratulations.

Curious beat.

IRIS

He studied Physics for two years at the
University. But after he came home from
overseas he couldn't really do much of
anything. He's a drug addict now. Once, on
April Fool's day, he pretended to hang
himself. And he nearly did.

Beat.

Are you at all familiar with the work of
Nikolai Lobachevsky?

LAWRENCE

Yes. No.

IRIS

Well, he introduced the idea that two parallel
lines could intersect, which is a constant
source of fascination for my father, but no
one else. If he brings up the subject, just do
what my mother does and pretend you smell
something burning in the kitchen. I'm a
Buddhist, by the way. Sister Anamelda says
that Catholicism is completely incompatible
with Buddhism, even though they both have
nuns. She has a very large boil on her eyelid,
so even when her eye is closed it looks like it's
still open. You wonder why God would do
something so ugly and cruel to such a
religious old woman. But who knows. Maybe
he actually has a sense of humour. Miss Rose
doesn't believe in God at all. Which is

extraordinary, because she's my godmother.
My father, by the way, doesn't even believe in
a soul. What about you, Mr. Lawrence?

LAWRENCE
I've been to hell.

IRIS
That must have been interesting.

LAWRENCE
I don't know what I believe.

IRIS
That wouldn't necessarily make you an
atheist; just indecisive. That's a ten-letter
word.

LAWRENCE
My hands feel like they're not attached.

IRIS
They seem to be. I hope you're warm enough.
I can get you a blanket if you like. Are you
aware that you have practically no hair on
your legs whatsoever. I believe that's a sign of
intelligence.

LAWRENCE
Not if you shave them it isn't.

IRIS
I never heard of a man shaving his legs
before. I'll have to write that down in my
diary. I'm keeping a complete record of
everything.
    Beat.

LAWRENCE
Why?

IRIS
> It's my father's idea, actually. He says that I
> ask too many questions. He says I should just
> write them down, because at some later date,
> I'll be able to answer them all myself. Tell me
> a little more about hell. Did you happen to
> see Father Wallace? He was our parish priest.
> He was quite controversial, but he died of
> emphysema.

LAWRENCE
> Where did you say your dad was, ma'am?

IRIS
> Well, like I told you—

> *Appearing from upstairs.*

OWEN
> Right here.

> *Beat.*

IRIS
> Look. A perfect stranger.

LAWRENCE
> Sir.

OWEN
> What's—going on?

IRIS
> I found him on the beach.

OWEN
> No kidding?

LAWRENCE
> Yeah. I'm—I—I'm—

IRIS

This is Mr. Lawrence. His hands feel like
they're not attached.

OWEN

What are you doing in that—bathrobe?

IRIS

It's yours.

OWEN

It is?

IRIS

It's quite the story.

OWEN

Why don't you let him tell it.

IRIS

My father wants me to take a vow of silence.

OWEN

No one likes a ten-year-old with an opinion.

IRIS

Especially a more interesting one.

OWEN

So. What's the, uh—what's the story?

LAWRENCE

Your daughter took all my clothes, sir.

OWEN

Sorry. Headache. Sorry. She, she what?

IRIS

He's looking for a room to rent.

OWEN

Is that right?

LAWRENCE
I—might be.

OWEN
Not sure?

IRIS
He's a poet.

OWEN
A poet.

LAWRENCE
I just—seem like one.

IRIS
And he's been to hell.

OWEN
What have you done with his clothes, Iris?

IRIS
They're wet.

OWEN
Where's my prescription got to? Hell?

IRIS
I believe you took them all.

OWEN
And why are your clothes wet? Is that
something I care to know?

LAWRENCE
I fell in the water.

OWEN
Oh, is that right?

LAWRENCE
It's very foggy out, Sir.

OWEN

Uh huh?

IRIS

I heard a splash.

LAWRENCE

Suddenly, everything disappeared underneath
me. It was—

OWEN

Would you mind not following me around the
room, Iris?

IRIS

My father is a recluse.

OWEN

So you needed a place to stay? Is that—? Is—
is—that—?

IRIS

We can put you in Mr. Lowell's old room. He
ran off with the Avon lady.

OWEN

That, of course, is not true. Excuse me. I have
to sit down. Sorry. You seem like a very nice—
man, Mr. Lawrence. A very nice, very straight
forward sort of, soaking wet sort of—and a
poet no less. That's—

LAWRENCE

Not—

OWEN

But we can't have you staying here, I'm afraid.
We—we just—we can't. Find me an aspirin.
Sorry. We don't take boarders anymore. It's—
it's—

LAWRENCE

I thought that might be the case.

OWEN

Yes. It's—yes—the case. Sorry.

IRIS

What about Miss Rose?

OWEN

She's—hardly a boarder. She's a family friend.
Well, friend is a—she's a long-time—I
shouldn't even say resident. That sounds a
little—

IRIS

She finds my father sexually attractive. Which
is extraordinary.

OWEN

You know the rule about using words that
have more letters than your age.

IRIS

(*to MR. LAWRENCE*) I'm not allowed to say
"senectitude" until after my birthday.

OWEN

Won't that be delightful?

Beat.

Even if we did have room, which we don't,
really—my wife isn't well. She's not, well—
she's—she's—well, she's just—she's—how
should I put this—she's—

IRIS

Not well.

OWEN

She's—thank you, Iris. Not well.

26

LAWRENCE

I heard she fell—down—the stairs and—
broke her wrist.

OWEN

It's actually a little more serious than that.

LAWRENCE

Oh, I'm sorry.

OWEN

It's a compound fracture. Iris, I wonder if you
could stop rolling your eyes to the back of
your head for a minute, and go and see if Mr.
Lawrence's clothes are dry. He must be
awfully, awfully anxious to get out of here. Are
you?

LAWRENCE

I was enjoying the visit.

OWEN

Oh.

LAWRENCE

She was telling me about her goldfish.

IRIS

Isn't it tragic?

OWEN

Yes. We were all pretty—broken up about it.

LAWRENCE

I guess he was quite the fish, then. Influential.

OWEN

What?

LAWRENCE

What?

IRIS

I don't think it's a coincidence that ever since
he was flushed down the toilet, American
warships have been steaming their way
towards Havana.

LAWRENCE

Stranger things have happened.

OWEN

Have they?

LAWRENCE

Have—haven't they?

OWEN

Look; if you don't mind, Mr. Lawrence, I
wonder if you could get out of my—bathrobe,
please. It's—(*MR. LAWRENCE complies*)—and
back into your own things if they're—hold
it—what are you—? Not here. Please.
(*Covering MR. LAWRENCE again*) Are you out
of your—? This is—

LAWRENCE

You said—

OWEN

I didn't mean—for God's sake! Please! Put
them—please.

LAWRENCE

Sorry.

OWEN

Good grief.

IRIS

My father is a bit of a prude.

OWEN

    I'm not.

LAWRENCE

    I understand.

IRIS

    Personally, I find the sight of male genitals
    extremely disappointing.

OWEN

    That's the last time I let anybody take you to a
    livestock show.

LAWRENCE

    You and me, we were in school together, or
    something.

OWEN

    What?

LAWRENCE

    Have I seen you before?

OWEN

    I doubt it. What are you—?

LAWRENCE

    What?

OWEN

    —talking about?

LAWRENCE

    Sometimes, I recognize people I haven't—you
    know?—met.

OWEN

    Uh, huh.

LAWRENCE

    It's just that—that—sometimes even the
    strangest, what do you call them?—

surroundings seem—to—to—yeah—or, or I find myself remembering things as they're—as—But I think that's just—a collision of molecules, like possibilities. Don't you? Or maybe an electrical impulse or something. Wires connecting the front part of the brain and—and uh—and I, I don't recall the rest.

Beat.

IRIS

I think you'll make a scintillating guest, Mr. Lawrence.

LAWRENCE

Is there somewhere I could—sit down? I feel as if I'm—drawing attention.

IRIS

Just make yourself completely at home.

OWEN

Excuse me. I'd like to have a word with my daughter. In the next room if you don't—

LAWRENCE

The next room. That's—

OWEN

Iris.

OWEN and IRIS start to leave and LAWRENCE follows.

OWEN

Where are you going?

LAWRENCE

What?

OWEN

Wait here.

LAWRENCE
     Where?

OWEN
     Just—

LAWRENCE
     Just—?

OWEN
     —the two of us.

LAWRENCE
     Right. Got it. Just—who? Us?

OWEN
     No. Us.

LAWRENCE
     (*Distressed*) I'm kind of unclear about where you want everybody to be at this point, sir.

OWEN
     I want you to stay here. Just—here. For the time being. We're going in there.

LAWRENCE
     Got it.

OWEN
     Good.

     OWEN drags IRIS from the room.

     MR. LAWRENCE stands obediently. After a moment, SYLVIA enters down the stairs, with a her wrist in a cast. Unseen by him, she passes by, in a bit of a daze.

SYLVIA
     It's late. Why don't you go upstairs to bed?

She exits. MR. LAWRENCE, turns around to find no one there.

He heads up the stairs, as directed. After a moment, SYLVIA returns, watching him go. IRIS and OWEN return from the kitchen. SYLVIA looks at OWEN. IRIS addresses at the audience.

IRIS

There are mysteries that happen. And you're just supposed to believe in them. In the Catholic Church, they train you up to something like the Holy Trinity, for example, by starting you off with easier stuff. Like St. Bernadette.

Lights change slowly; morning. IRIS wraps a tea towel around her head, nun-style. On the radio, reports of the Cuban crisis.

She was visited by The Virgin Mary and given a piece of paper with some kind of important information on it, which the Pope saw, but he was so shocked that he said he would never read it out loud. To anyone.

IRIS serves MR. LAWRENCE coffee. He really likes the sugar.

IRIS

Miss Rose says she knows what's on it. It's the date the world ends.

LAWRENCE

Is that right?

SYLVIA shuts off the radio.

IRIS

> She said, once, she would trade her very soul
> for one of those chocolate bottles with
> Drambuie in it. To the surprise of no one.

SYLVIA

> That's—sugar; Mr. Lawrence.

LAWRENCE

> What did I say just now?

SYLVIA

> I don't—think you said anything. I just said,
> "That's sugar."

LAWRENCE

> Oh.

> *Beat.*

LAWRENCE

> And what did I say?

IRIS

> Sometimes, before she goes to work in the
> morning, she sneaks a couple of swigs of rye,
> from the bottle in her wardrobe. I hate to be
> rude, but she should wait to do that until
> after she's applied her lipstick.

SYLVIA

> She's making all this up.

IRIS

> Why would I make up a thing like that?

SYLVIA

> What's—in this coffee?

IRIS

> Isn't it revolutionary? Why did you shave off
> your moustache this morning, Mr. Lawrence?

33

SYLVIA
Curiosity killed the cat. Isn't that right, Mr.
Lawrence?

LAWRENCE
I'm sorry; I wasn't—

IRIS
Frankly, I thought it was just Miss Rose's
armpit hair in the sink.

SYLVIA
What time is it?

IRIS
She didn't drain the tub, as usual. Would you
like another coffee, Mr. Lawrence?

LAWRENCE
Sure.

IRIS
I just take mine black, of course.

SYLVIA
Why aren't you in school this morning?

IRIS
Sister Anamelda says that I have to renounce
Buddhism completely before I can return to
class.

SYLVIA
In other words, you haven't done your
homework.

IRIS
Do you know what Zen is, Mr. Lawrence?

SYLVIA
Does he look Oriental to you?

IRIS

We used to have a Chinese man living with us.
He burned incense in a dish.

SYLVIA

Poor soul.

IRIS

You should have just heard the way he said
"chrysanthemum."

SYLVIA

Iris.

IRIS

We used to buy bunches of them just so he
would say the word.

LAWRENCE

Chrysanthemum.

IRIS

Chrysanthemum.

SYLVIA

He worked so hard to bring his wife and his
son over. Wanted to get himself a bungalow in
the valley somewhere. Start a little chicken
farm.

IRIS

You have very interesting markings.

LAWRENCE

Thank you.

SYLVIA

Some people don't like immigrants, but I do.
Each wave of newcomers. Like the rings on a
tree. Iris, I'm sure Mr. Lawrence is quite
aware of how interesting his markings are.

IRIS
    It's uncanny.

SYLVIA
    Is she making you nervous?

LAWRENCE
    I think it's just—the radio.

SYLVIA
    It's not—on

    A beat.

LAWRENCE
    Yeah.

IRIS
    Mr. Lawrence is a poet.

SYLVIA
    Oh?

LAWRENCE
    So I hear.

IRIS
    I told him all about Amahl, of course.

LAWRENCE
    Yeah.

SYLVIA
    That stupid fish. She took the damn thing
    everywhere. Even to high mass.

IRIS
    You said damn.

SYLVIA
    No I didn't.

IRIS
    I loved him. Mr. Lawrence.

LAWRENCE

Could you—get another one?

IRIS

(*Dramatically, throwing herself about*) Oh, no; I couldn't do that. I simply couldn't. That would be too ironic.

SYLVIA

What a—lunatic. Poor Miss Rose is scared to death of her.

IRIS

She's afraid I'll find out her secret, is why. She's in league with the devil.

SYLVIA

No she isn't.

IRIS

She bathes in lavender bubble bath so she can disguise the aroma of Satan. That's what you said.

SYLVIA

Take that towel off your head.

IRIS

It's just like the smell of fish guts.

LAWRENCE

I didn't know that.

IRIS

She tries to seduce my father all the time. You should see the way they carried on at New Year's. It was revolting.

SYLVIA

Would you like some breakfast, Mr. Lawrence?
I can't do much with my left hand, but then I
never could.

IRIS

Are you flirting, mother?

LAWRENCE

Should I be on my way, now?

IRIS

No.

SYLVIA

Where?

IRIS

You can't go.

SYLVIA

What about your things? Exactly.

OWEN

(*Appearing*) If the man wants to leave, it isn't
right to try and stop him.

SYLVIA

He hasn't got a place to stay.

IRIS

Isn't it tragic?

OWEN

What are you doing up?

SYLVIA

Tell her to go to school.

She exits to the kitchen.

OWEN

Go to school.

> *No reaction to his half-hearted command. She*
> *coughs a little fake cough.*

OWEN

I see my wife is feeling much better this morning. You must be having quite a positive influence on her. Clothes not dry yet?

IRIS

Someone stole them off the line. Will wonders never cease?

OWEN

Really?

IRIS

Mother said he looks better in your bathrobe than you do.

> *Beat.*

My father never shaves.

> *OWEN makes his way over to his drafting table.*

OWEN

Go to school, Iris.

IRIS

I have pneumonia.

OWEN

Is that right?

IRIS

Sister Anamelda called me a heretic.

OWEN

So was Galileo.

IRIS

Mr. Lawrence has to promise to be here when I get back.

OWEN

I'm sure he has better things to do than hang around here all day. (*Without looking up*) Where is it you're headed to, exactly?

LAWRENCE

Headed to? Headed to. *echo*

IRIS

You're welcome to stay with us, of course.

OWEN

He can't. He—he can't.

IRIS

Why not?

OWEN

Because.

IRIS

Because isn't an answer.

OWEN

Who said it wasn't?

IRIS

You did.

OWEN

Oh, suddenly you're listening.

IRIS

He said, "Because isn't an answer," and I said, "Why," and he said, "Because."

OWEN

People have lives to get on with. Isn't that right, Mr. Lawrence. Who knows? Maybe he has a—a dental appointment.

IRIS

Really, father. How jejune. *Lacking nutritive value insipid uninteresting*

SYLVIA enters with breakfast.

OWEN
    Don't use that word.

IRIS
    It's only six letters.

OWEN
    You don't even know what it means.

SYLVIA
    Do you have a dental appointment, Mr.
    Lawrence?

LAWRENCE
    Not to speak of. My teeth are—

OWEN
    I was making a point. He can't wander
    around, forever, in my bathrobe.

SYLVIA
    He can wear some of your everyday things.

OWEN
    They'd hardly—they wouldn't—fit.

SYLVIA
    You don't wear them.

OWEN
    I —do. I—most certainly—I—

IRIS
    Mr. Lawrence should get a job at the cannery.

LAWRENCE
    The cannery? *echo*

SYLVIA
    That's a good idea.

41

OWEN

The cannery? The cannery.

LAWRENCE shrugs.

SYLVIA

A man needs to keep himself busy, isn't that right? Otherwise—what happens?

OWEN

I don't know. What happens?

SYLVIA

He loses his sense of purpose.

OWEN

Is that right? Is that—? His sense of purpose. Where'd you get that? *Reader's Digest?*

SYLVIA

When a man loses his sense of purpose; that's tragic.

OWEN

Tragic.

SYLVIA

Breakfast?

OWEN

No thank you.

SYLVIA

I wasn't asking you.

OWEN

In that case, I'll have toast.

SYLVIA

Make it yourself. I have a broken wrist.

Music.

Lawrence functions as a catalyst

IRIS

(*Out, as the rest disappear*) My father's not
pleased one bit. Like most people, he wants
things to be just the way they always were.

> *Beat.*

Trouble is, they never really were.

> *MISS ROSE appears, smoking, reading a
> magazine.*

ROSE

There are certain skills required to work at a
fish-packing plant, you know.

IRIS

I forgot. What are they again?

ROSE

And incidentally, there's no such thing as
destiny.

IRIS

How would you know?

ROSE

Experience.

If you want friends, dearie, you should work
on your popularity, instead of trolling the
beaches at night for vagrants.

IRIS

I'm popular enough.

ROSE

Really?

IRIS

I'm in the school orchestra, for your
information.

43

ROSE

Playing the triangle won't make you a lot of
friends, hon.

IRIS

That was dad's idea.

ROSE

When I was your age, I took up the bassoon.
Men are only impressed by anything louder
than they are.

IRIS

Mr. Lawrence isn't just a friend.

ROSE

No?

IRIS

Have you noticed how far apart his eyes are?

ROSE

I haven't met the man.

IRIS

Mother calls him the inscrutable Mr.
Lawrence.

ROSE

I'll bet she does.

IRIS

It must be kind of sad for you, I was thinking,
that my mother isn't leaving for the time
being. Since you're secretly in love with my
father. It could have worked out quite well for
you.

ROSE

He's not my type.

*Iris is Matchmaking Sylvia + Lawrence
Rose + Owen*

44

Beginning of a thesis
How Iris & Rose work
against one another onstage

Act I
Act II Godmother

IRIS

Remember that New Year's party, when you passed the orange? I hate to say it, but that was humiliating to everyone.

ROSE

That's what happens when you stay up past your bedtime.

IRIS

Sister Anamelda says that divorce is a cardinal sin. So if you happen to have sex with a Catholic, even if he's separated from his wife, that makes you an adulteress. If she died, see, then it would be okay to have sex or whatever, except that when he got to heaven, he'd have to go back with his original wife at least three days a week. Cocktail?

ROSE

The last one you made nearly unraveled my hairdo. And not too much ice.

IRIS

Why do you wear it up like that, anyway? Is it true what my mother says? That you're hopelessly stuck in the war years.

ROSE

Don't you have some school work to do?

IRIS

Actually, that's one of the advantages of an atomic bomb attack, Miss Rose. You don't have to bother memorizing the trading posts of the Hudson's Bay Company.

ROSE

I can think of another advantage.

IRIS

Me, too. We'll have to go down into an air-raid shelter. Imagine. We'll all be crammed in there together. Our legs rubbing up against each other and everything. You and father. Mother and Mr. Lawrence. You should just see the way she looks at him. Not in a disgusting way or anything. Just the way she stares at him. I think she knows.

ROSE

What?

IRIS

I can't go into it at length, at the moment.

ROSE

Really?

IRIS

I have to do some more investigating, first.

ROSE

Just stay out of my dresser drawers; you never know what might be in them.

IRIS

Believe me; I know.

ROSE

You wouldn't want to lose a hand.

IRIS

Do you smell—fresh halibut somewhere?

Beat.

Excuse me.

She runs off. ROSE sniffs her hand; goes to make herself a drink. MR. LAWRENCE enters, unnoticed, and watches her. He's holding a

pair of scissors, in the other hand a newspaper
clipping which he pockets. As she turns back
towards him, she studies him for a beat.

LAWRENCE
Ma'am.

ROSE
The new boarder. Your eyes aren't very far
apart at all.

LAWRENCE
Thank you.

ROSE
I'm in the room just down the hall. Miss Rose.

Maybe I'll tell you my first name when we've
known each other a little longer.

Beat.   time Lapse or irony

ROSE
Vivian. Care for a rye and ginger?

LAWRENCE
O—O.K.

ROSE
I suppose that delightful little—thing has
already told you lots and lots about me.

LAWRENCE
Who?

ROSE
The girl. She likes to make up stories to
entertain herself. They ought to buy a
television if you ask me. Sad truth is, they
can't afford it. He can't work, poor thing—
and she delivers the *Star Weekly.*   Toronto

LAWRENCE
Where did we meet?

ROSE
I don't think we have, honey.

She hands him a drink.

Those aren't your pants, are they?

LAWRENCE
Not these particular ones, no.

ROSE
Uh, huh.

Beat.

LAWRENCE
I'm not—What's supposed to happen now?

ROSE

Seductive

I'm sure if we stand here long enough, we'll think of something.

LAWRENCE
Could I have one of those?

ROSE
Cigarette?

LAWRENCE
Please.

ROSE
Sure, hon.

LAWRENCE
Normally I don't smoke, but you make it look kind of—

Beat.

ROSE
Thank you.

He downs the entire drink.

ROSE

My.

LAWRENCE

Eventually I'll come to feel more and more at home here.

ROSE

Sure.

LAWRENCE

At the moment, I'm a little—uncomfortable. You know? I think it's just the walls. They seem kind of—kind of—

ROSE

Do they?

LAWRENCE

Yeah.

ROSE

Relax.

Beat. He attempts to smoke.

LAWRENCE

I hope to get a job at the cannery down the road, maybe.

ROSE

So I gather.

LAWRENCE

I'm not really familiar with that line of work.

ROSE

No?

LAWRENCE

I understand you have to wear a hairnet,
though. I understand that's part of the—job.

ROSE

There's a little more to it than that.

LAWRENCE

Right. What?

ROSE

Where are you from, exactly?

LAWRENCE

Oh, all over, I guess. East of here. North—of
here. Other places, too. Cold places. Other—
other—you know—

ROSE

Right.

LAWRENCE

places.

ROSE

Right.

LAWRENCE

Places that I left but they didn't—they
didn't—didn't—

ROSE

What's wrong?

LAWRENCE

I'm feeling a little—

ROSE

Maybe it's the cigarette.

Taking the cigarette, she extinguishes it.

LAWRENCE
Oh.

ROSE
Maybe you should start with a lighter brand
and work your way up.

LAWRENCE
Excuse me, ma'am. (*Starting off*) I'm going to
have to go up to my room, if you don't mind,
and make myself—perpendicular.

ROSE
That's my specialty, Mr. Lawrence. I used to
take blood for the Red Cross.

She helps him off.

IRIS
(*Appearing around a corner*) She's trying
corrupt his soul, of course. Luckily, when she
took him up to his room and tried to undress
him, he passed out with his pants around his
ankles.

SYLVIA
Red Cross?

IRIS
Don't worry; nothing happened.

SYLVIA
I wasn't asking. Was I asking?

OWEN
(*Appearing*) There is something not quite
right about the man. I just—

IRIS
Where do things go after they're flushed?

51

SYLVIA

The only thing she ever nursed was a drink.
Don't go repeating that.

IRIS

Where do things go after they're flushed?

OWEN

The sewer.

SYLVIA

He hasn't been with us half a day and she's
got him undressed.

IRIS

Where does the sewer go?

SYLVIA

The sea.

OWEN

He was undressed when he arrived.

IRIS

Do you remember the markings Amahl had
on the left side of his head? Well, Mr.
Lawrence happens to have exactly the same
ones on his neck in exactly the same spot.
Well, not exactly the same spot. Fish don't
have necks.

SYLVIA

What?

IRIS

Do I have to spell it out.

SYLVIA

Go somewhere.

OWEN

(*Into his work*) You think he might be an
escaped lunatic? Just a question.

IRIS

Don't you see?

OWEN

He's a little—a little—

SYLVIA

What?

OWEN

Extraordinary.

SYLVIA

It's part of his charm.

OWEN

Oh. Charm. Is that what that is? I didn't—

IRIS

Remember when you said there was
something fishy about him?

OWEN

Still, it wouldn't hurt to phone around to a
few—you know—local—

SYLVIA

What?

OWEN

Asylums?

SYLVIA

Not everybody who's peculiar is insane,
Owen.

> *A look to IRIS.*

IRIS

And Miss Rose, when she took him upstairs,
said he was looking a little green around the
gills?

SYLVIA

He's a poet.

OWEN

Robert W. Service never walked off the end of
a pier.

IRIS listens, without moving.

SYLVIA

What would you know about it? Have you ever
written a poem?

OWEN

Has he?

SYLVIA

You took one look at the man and decided
you didn't like him.

OWEN

Why would I write a poem?

SYLVIA

Why wouldn't you?

OWEN

And, by the way, what do you call this?

SYLVIA

What?

OWEN

This.

SYLVIA

A desk?

OWEN

This. What could be more poetic, in its own way, than a rhomboid? Well, alright, not a rhomboid.

SYLVIA

Is something burning in the kitchen?

She gets up and goes toward the kitchen.

OWEN

Sure. I get it.

Stopping.

SYLVIA

Geometry is fine, Owen. But what are you pursuing? In the real world?

OWEN

Pursuing? Gee, I didn't know we were all pursuing something. I guess I forgot to read the instruction manual on a meaningful life.

IRIS

There's a manual?

OWEN

Why don't I go down and apply at the cannery? That's pretty meaningful work.

SYLVIA

Why did your father ever leave you this house?

OWEN

I've seen enough of the real world.

SYLVIA

Lots of men went overseas, Owen. And lots of them came back.

OWEN

You think I don't have ambition? Fine—
aspiration?

SYLVIA

When have you ever been up before noon?

OWEN

To find you, in a heap at the bottom of the
stairs. Is it any wonder I sleep in?

SYLVIA

Sorry.

OWEN

That is my suitcase.

SYLVIA

Sorry.

OWEN

If you leave me I'll have—nothing.

SYLVIA

You have this—house.

OWEN

Sylvia—

SYLVIA

At the moment I have a broken wrist. So it's
not easy to pack a bag.

IRIS

It's still packed.

SYLVIA

Iris.

OWEN

Please.

SYLVIA

I am not having this conversation.

OWEN

What conversation?

SYLVIA

"Am I going or am I staying."

OWEN

I don't want to have that conversation.

SYLVIA

Of course not.

OWEN

Do you want to have that conversation?

SYLVIA

No.

OWEN

Then why are we having it?

SYLVIA

We're not.

OWEN

We're not?

SYLVIA

We're not.

OWEN

Good.

SYLVIA

Good.

IRIS

Good.

They look at each other.

Music: "Stranger on the Shore." Above them,
MR. LAWRENCE quietly freaks out.

Later; Miss Rose is going out again.

ROSE

He could be a Russian spy for all we know.

IRIS

Could be.

ROSE

Lawrence. What kind of a name is Lawrence?

IRIS

It's not Russian.

ROSE

He wouldn't use his Russian name.

OWEN

What happened to his clothes? That's what I
want to know.

ROSE

Barely speaks the language.

SYLVIA

There are—many—many—explanations for a
man who arrives, naked, in the middle of the
night.

Beat.

Excuse me.

She exits.

ROSE

A submarine could have dropped him off up
the coast. Happens all the time.

IRIS

It does?

OWEN
> What would he be spying on here?

ROSE
> That's the big question, isn't it? If anybody
> wants me, I'll be at the legion.
>
> *ROSE exits.*

IRIS
> Try not to drink too much, Miss Rose. My
> mother says it makes you promiscuous.
>
> *Lights change. She speaks to the audience.*
>
> Every night, Miss Rose goes off to the legion,
> to drink rye and ginger ale, and neck with all
> the veterans, and pretend it's V.E. Day, over
> and over again. Meanwhile, my mother isn't
> going anywhere. She doesn't realize it yet, but
> Mr. Lawrence is bringing the whole world
> back into balance. Even Mr. Kruschev is
> having second thoughts.

SYLVIA
> Stop it.
>
> *SYLVIA tries to read her book.*

IRIS
> So you don't believe in reincarnation?

SYLVIA
> You want to be excommunicated?

IRIS
> Martin Luther was excommunicated.

SYLVIA
> Did your father tell you that?

IRIS
> Mama.

Trying to put her head in her mother's lap.

SYLVIA

Quit acting like a child.

IRIS

I am a child.

SYLVIA

Honestly. (*Noticing*) What's this?

IRIS

What?

SYLVIA

Hold still.

IRIS

Don't.

SYLVIA

Have you been pulling your hair out again?
There's a little bald patch right in the middle
of your head.

IRIS

It's a sign of intelligence.

SYLVIA

By the way, I had a word with Sister Lillian
this morning. She says you've been telling all
sorts of preposterous stories.

IRIS

More preposterous, say, than the immaculate
conception?

SYLVIA

Get off me. You're too old for this.

60

IRIS

Are you aware, mother, that he's been in the bathroom for nearly an hour?

SYLVIA

So?

IRIS

He might not know his way around in there.

SYLVIA

Well, he can't very well flush himself down the toilet, can he?

Beat.

IRIS

(*Out*) She has no idea what's going on. She didn't seem even slightly bothered by the way he ate dinner, tonight. She overfed him, of course.

It's a common mistake with goldfish.

MR. LAWRENCE enters.

IRIS

Are you alright, Mr. Lawrence?

LAWRENCE

Why?

IRIS

We were terribly worried about you. My mother especially.

SYLVIA

No I wasn't.

LAWRENCE

I couldn't get the—fan turned on.

SYLVIA
Fan?

IRIS
That's because there isn't one.

Beat.

LAWRENCE
Well I wish I'd known that.

SYLVIA
What have you done to your eyebrows, now?

IRIS
Mr. Lawrence, you become more interesting by the minute.

LAWRENCE
Is it too much?

SYLVIA
For what?

LAWRENCE
I was—I was—what?

SYLVIA
Pardon?

LAWRENCE
Is that—is that a—good book, ma'am?

SYLVIA
What? This?

IRIS
My mother only pretends to read.

SYLVIA
I can't get past—page one.

LAWRENCE
Is it a mystery?

SYLVIA

    The rest of it is.

LAWRENCE

    I used to read, but you know what words are like.

SYLVIA

    I can never bear to know what happens. It always seems to turn out—badly for someone.

    Beat. He looks at her with deep curiosity.

IRIS

    How long can you hold your breath underwater, Mr. Lawrence?

SYLVIA

    Isn't there some homework you're not doing?

IRIS

    I think I already told you, mother, but I have no interest in an academic career. I'm going to Tibet.

SYLVIA

    Did you practice your instrument?

IRIS

    Would anybody like a gimlet?

LAWRENCE

    Yes—please.

SYLVIA

    No.

LAWRENCE

    No.

    Long beat. SYLVIA and MR. LAWRENCE look at one another, as IRIS watches.

    Tibet?

SYLVIA

There are these two old smelt-fishermen on
the beach. One of them is blind and the
other one wears a woman's hat. She hangs
around pestering them all the time, and they
put stupid ideas into her head. As if she
doesn't have enough of her own.

IRIS

Mr. Lawrence believes in reincarnation. Don't
you, Mr. Lawrence?

LAWRENCE

It seems like a good idea.

SYLVIA

It does, doesn't it? It seems like a very good
idea

IRIS

Catholics are only supposed to believe in
heaven, Mr. Lawrence. But who wants to
spend eternity with Pope Pius XII and Dag
Hammerskjold?

SYLVIA

I think everyone deserves another chance at
life.

LAWRENCE

To exonerate themselves.

SYLVIA

That's right.

LAWRENCE

What does that mean? I just said that.

SYLVIA

It sounds about right.

LAWRENCE

You're already kind of perfect the way you are; it seems to me, ma'am.

SYLVIA

Because you don't know me.

LAWRENCE

Yeah?

OWEN enters and goes to his table.

SYLVIA

I'd like to come back as a—as a—what? I'd like to come back as—

OWEN

Who's been cutting things out of the paper?

SYLVIA

I'd just like to come back, Mr. Lawrence.

SYLVIA leaves.

OWEN

Why? Where's she going?

IRIS

When she dies.

OWEN

Dies?

He looks at them through a cut hole in the paper.

IRIS

In my next life, I'm coming back as a member of the Royal Family.

OWEN

>Apparently, my daughter got the wrong end
>of the stick, Mr. Lawrence. She and Princess
>Anne were somehow mixed up at birth.

IRIS

>Isn't it tragic? I don't love my parents any less
>for it. As a matter of fact, I think I love them
>more. Poor things. Imagine having to live
>your entire life in a boarding house near a
>cannery.

OWEN

>You do.

IRIS

>May I touch your skin?

LAWRENCE

>O.K.

IRIS

>It's quite scaly, isn't it?

OWEN

>Go to bed. You're making everyone insane.
>Pardon me. I didn't mean insane. Not—
>literally.

IRIS

>I have a new bedtime, for your information.

OWEN

>You know what happens when little girls don't
>get their sleep. Their skin wrinkles and falls
>off in chunks. Don't take my word for it, look
>it up.

IRIS

>I did.

OWEN

Take your chances.

Beat.

IRIS

I must speak to you in the morning, Mr.
Lawrence. On an urgent matter regarding
your past.

LAWRENCE blanches.

IRIS

Good night, everyone.

She exits.

OWEN

I knew we shouldn't have ordered that
encyclopedia. What good is being a parent if
you can't misinform your children?

IRIS

(*Reappearing to the audience*) I'm going to have
to keep an eye on Mr. Lawrence. He doesn't
seem to be adjusting very normally to a life of
oxygen.

LAWRENCE

Why do you draw all those shapes?

OWEN

I have an obsessive preoccupation with angles.
Evidence of my social deterioration.

LAWRENCE

They're—beautiful. Kind of.

OWEN

Thank you.

Pause.

OWEN

> You haven't told us a whole lot about yourself since you've been here.

LAWRENCE

> No.

> *Beat.*

OWEN

> Well—the most disappointing thing you can know about a person, sometimes, is the truth.

> *Beat.*

> There's an epidemic of curiosity these days. I don't mean a thirst for knowledge. That would be—No. It's not the big questions. Whatever those are. It's the insipid details. "Does she or doesn't she?" "How Green Was My Valley?" "Is he an escaped mental patient?" Ridiculous. Isn't it ridiculous? It is. It's—why did you tell my daughter you'd been to hell?

> *Beat.*

> Did this hell involve wrist restraints of any kind?

LAWRENCE

> (*Getting closer*) You studied physics, once.

OWEN

> Not really. Not—I dropped out, I—Aside from my obscure interest in geometry, I have no aptitude for anything. At all. I left college and joined the army.

> *LAWRENCE touches the drawing.*

OWEN

    Please don't—

He withdraws his hand.

LAWRENCE

    This looks like a spine, I think. Or a prison of
some kind. These bars.

OWEN

    It isn't really supposed to be anything.

LAWRENCE

    You were wounded I hear.

OWEN

    Uh huh. Well, rifle loading was never one of
my—wounded in action was the—uh—
official—people talk about shooting
themselves in the foot. But I—yes sirree. I—
I—and then of course I spent the rest of the
war on morphine. Fantastic, really. I didn't
know who won until 1946. I was decorated for
bravery. Isn't that—? You're—wearing a bit
of—make-up, I see.

    *MR. LAWRENCE's hand moves from the table to
OWEN's face, touching him, and studying him.*

OWEN

    What are you—? Mr. Lawrence, what, what are
you—? This is—I think, perhaps, a little too—
poetic for me.

    *LAWRENCE drops his hand away; mortified by
his own behaviour.*

LAWRENCE

    Your eyes, sir.

OWEN

Uh huh?

LAWRENCE

I saw them glistening, kind of sadly, I thought.

OWEN

Glistening?

LAWRENCE

Isn't that a word? Sometimes, I don't know what's a word and what isn't.

OWEN

It's a—it's a word. It's a—

LAWRENCE

What is it you're trying to draw, sir?

OWEN

I—I don't know. Actually. It's really just abstract—you know—lines.

LAWRENCE

Lines?

OWEN

Lines. Just—

LAWRENCE

Tell me why you're so sad.

OWEN

Sad? I'm not—sad. I'm—not happy, certainly. But hardly—

Beat.

I find happy people suspect. Frankly. My wife is a happy person by nature. Was. It was always kind of annoying the way she looked on the bright side of everything. But she's lived with

me long enough to know that there isn't one.
Not here. Not—now.

LAWRENCE
Why don't you escape, then?

OWEN
It's a question of—a question of—getting
organized. You can't just up and—anyway, I
don't think escape is the—what exactly is it
you want, Mr. Lawrence? From us? This isn't
about having a place to stay, is it? What is this
about?

LAWRENCE
I'd like to be part of something that isn't—

OWEN
Isn't what?

LAWRENCE
Me.

OWEN
What is it?

LAWRENCE recoils. Music.

OWEN
What's wrong?

LAWRENCE
Everything is moving, kind of.

OWEN
Is it?

LAWRENCE
Isn't it?

IRIS

(*Reading from an encyclopedia*) An organ
running along the outside length of their
bodies and parts of their heads tell fish
exactly what's going on around them, even if
they can't see it. It's called the lateral line
system. Like a sixth sense. It gives fish a sense
of movement as they swim and helps them
orient themselves. It consists of hair-like
sensors. (*out*) Mr. Lawrence should never
have shaved off his moustache.

LAWRENCE

I have to—have to—go somewhere, and—
and—what?

OWEN

Mr. Lawrence?

He wanders away as OWEN watches him.

After a moment, SYLVIA enters.

SYLVIA

What are you doing up?

She puts on the radio. Music.

Where's our guest?

OWEN

What?

SYLVIA

The inscrutable Mr. Lawrence.

OWEN

Let's see. That's right. He's gone bananas.

SYLVIA

What do you mean?

72

OWEN
Last time I saw him, he was babbling
incoherently, um—seeing things, and, well,
being sort of inappropriately affectionate.

SYLVIA
What are you talking about?

OWEN
He—touched me.

SYLVIA
Where?

OWEN
Not there.

SYLVIA
He's spontaneous.

OWEN
Is he?

SYLVIA
I like that.

OWEN
Why? You never liked it before. You never,
ever liked it before. Spontaneous? You were
perfectly happy until—when was that?—
yesterday.

SYLVIA
What gave you that idea?

OWEN
Content, then. You were content.

SYLVIA
I wasn't content, either.

OWEN

I'm running out of words here, Sylvia.
Mollified?

SYLVIA

—

OWEN

You must have been something.

Beat.

Twelve years?

SYLVIA

I don't know what I was. I didn't really think
about it. You know how you don't really think
about something? Ever? Then all of a sudden,
"blip." You think about it?

OWEN

"Blip"?

SYLVIA

Like a little bubble; I don't know. A bubble.

OWEN

A bubble is more like "bloop," isn't it?

SYLVIA

Bloop. Blip. You think about it.

OWEN

Is this from that book you're not reading?

SYLVIA

I'm capable of having a thought of my own,
you know. I used to have thoughts of my own
all the time.

OWEN

Twelve years, Sylvia. There must have been—a moment of—something bordering on satisfaction.

SYLVIA

Is that what you want?

OWEN

We hardly ever argue.

SYLVIA

We hardly ever speak, Owen.

OWEN

We're incompatible; that's all. I know you hate geometrical comparisons, but—consider what happens when two lines run parallel.

SYLVIA

Did I leave something on the—?

OWEN

Given time—there's a curve. A curve. Let me show you.

SYLVIA

I'll just—something's—

She goes off. He sits, empty. IRIS comes forward and stands behind her father, watching him for a moment as he drops his head into his hands. Suddenly he stops.

IRIS

I was watching you cry. It was rather interesting.

OWEN

(*Getting up*) I wasn't crying.

IRIS

    I'd like to make a note of it in my journal
    anyway.

OWEN

    (*Going*) Go somewhere. For God's sake, just—
    And take Mr. Lawrence with you.

IRIS

    Dad. He's here to help us.

OWEN

    Help us what? `

        Exits.

IRIS

    I know it's hard for you to believe because
    you don't believe in anything. But it's true all
    the same. He's going to bring this family
    together again.

ROSE

    (*Appearing, a little drunk*) Who is?

IRIS

    Our guest.

ROSE

    Uh, huh. And how's he going to do that, doll?

IRIS

    Is that—liquor I smell on your breath?

ROSE

    What makes you such a little smarty-pants,
    dearie?

IRIS

    I'm not really that smart, Miss Rose. I
    probably just seem that way to people who
    aren't.

ROSE

We'll see about that. Your precious Mr.
Lawrence is going to be found out for one
thing.

IRIS

He hasn't done anything.

ROSE

I don't like the way he looks at me.

IRIS

Don't you mean doesn't look at you?

ROSE

Did you tell him some horrible little story?

IRIS

Just that you were kind of—you know—evil.

ROSE

You better pray your brazen little heart out
that your mother doesn't leave. Because it'll
be just you and me then, doll. You—and me.
And I don't particularly like you.

IRIS

Nobody else does, either.

ROSE

But I intend to do something about it.

She goes. IRIS makes a little entry in her diary.

IRIS

(*Out*) I know for sure that these are last few
days of my childhood. I'm already beginning
to feel nostalgic about when I was nine. As the
rain begins to fall tonight, Miss Rose trips her
way up the stairs, and stumbles into her room.
The light goes off. Then I see Mr. Lawrence

standing in his bedroom window, completely
undressed, having some kind of nightmare;
except he's awake. I'm standing across the
street, now, under a tree. The rain falls harder
and harder. Harder than it's ever fallen, ever.
Tonight, it seems, the whole world might be
washed down the gutter. If I squint my eyes he
looks a little like he used to in his bowl.
Except that my mother is standing behind
him now. In another window, my father
stands, eyes closed, and dreams for a
moment, then opens the window wide and
leans out for air; his head wet and dripping
with rain. I'd call out to him, but it's such a
long time ago. He closes the window, shuts
the drapes. The light goes off and everything
is dark, now, except the one window where
I'm sitting, all those years ago, breathing fog
onto the glass, to write my name, backwards,
over and over again.

Sounds underwater.

BLACKOUT.

Act Two

*The following morning. MR. LAWRENCE is
dressed in clothes that aren't his. Iris has a
plant sprayer.*

LAWRENCE

So. What did you do with my—other—with
my—?

IRIS

I thought it was best to get rid of your other
clothes, Mr. Lawrence. Entirely.

LAWRENCE

Yeah?

IRIS

I don't know where you found that shirt, for
instance, but I think it was from a prison.

LAWRENCE

What makes you think that?

IRIS

It said "prison" on it.

LAWRENCE

Is—is that—is that—yeah?

IRIS

Even I was suspicious at first, until I figured
out who you really were.

LAWRENCE

A f—a fish?

IRIS

Isn't it surreal?

LAWRENCE

Have you told anyone else?

IRIS

You think they'd believe me for a second?

She squirts him with a bit of water.

LAWRENCE

So you didn't—What are you—?

IRIS

This should keep you fairly moist.

LAWRENCE

What is it?

IRIS

We don't want you drying up.

LAWRENCE

That's—thanks.

Beat.

IRIS

Poor Mr. Lawrence. The pressure must be
quite different out here.

LAWRENCE

Pressure.

IRIS

Do you find it a little uncomfortable, in the open air?

LAWRENCE

—

IRIS

You just have to learn how to fit in—that's all. Here.

LAWRENCE

What is it?

IRIS

One of my father's prescription pills. He says they make him feel more human.

LAWRENCE

They tried to—make me take things before.

IRIS

Who did?

LAWRENCE

What?

IRIS

Somebody tried to make you take things?

LAWRENCE

Did they?

IRIS

It was probably just a dream you were having; when you were a fish.

LAWRENCE

A dream? Yeah. Maybe I am a fish. That would—be—So, what happens now?

IRIS

Just try to act like a normal person.

LAWRENCE
    Sure. I can—

IRIS
    Like, maybe smoke a pipe or something.
    Where's the bowtie I gave you?

LAWRENCE
    Was that what that was?

    SYLVIA, entering, stops abruptly.

SYLVIA
    Good morning, Mr. Lawrence. Did you—sleep
    well?

LAWRENCE
    I—I—I—I—

SYLVIA
    Well, that's—that's—

LAWRENCE
    Uh—uh—

SYLVIA
    We're out of Coffee-mate at the moment;
    we'll just have to use—milk. Or—

    She exits.

IRIS
    Don't let your mouth hang open like that. It's
    why you have lips. By the way, Miss Rose is
    onto you. She thinks you're a communist spy,
    because your name doesn't seem Russian at
    all. And my father called an insane asylum
    this morning to find out if anyone was
    missing. He's probably just upset because he
    happens to know my mother was in your
    room last night.

LAWRENCE
> H—How?

IRIS
> There's no privacy in this house whatsoever.

LAWRENCE
> She wanted to talk. And—and—and—

IRIS
> My father is pretty conservative.

LAWRENCE
> He's just trying to figure things out, you
> know, by understanding—what?—the lines.
> The—lines. Or—or—you know?

IRIS
> You're terribly naïve, Mr. Lawrence. It's
> charming, at the moment. But you'll find it
> wears thin after a while. What?

LAWRENCE
> Is that a cushion over there?

IRIS
> Yes.

LAWRENCE
> I thought so.

> *She addresses the audience, as LAWRENCE
> exits.*

IRIS

> Mr. DaSilva said there's as much chance of
> your dead goldfish showing up at your house
> as anything else that ever happened. Who
> knew Shelley Fabares could sing?

> *She flips herself upside down.*

This could very well be the last day of my childhood. Even upside down things are losing their magic.

> *Car horn. MISS ROSE puts on her coat.*

IRIS

Rough night last night?

ROSE

Never trust a sailor, dearie.

IRIS

I'll make a note of that.

ROSE

I'm off.

> *Up-righting herself.*

IRIS

Miss Rose has left for work, this morning, with such a bad hangover that there's lipstick smeared all the way up inside her nostrils. Mr. Lawrence, meanwhile, was kind of upset that I found out his secret. Let's face it, who wants to be a fish? Especially one with so much responsibility on his shoulders? Well, fish don't have shoulders, but Mr. Lawrence does. Imagine.

> *SYLVIA appears with coffee, finding MR. LAWRENCE not there.*

SYLVIA

Why aren't you in school?

IRIS

(*Heading out*) I think it's the Feast of something.

SYLVIA

Don't be sacrilegious.

IRIS exits as OWEN enters in pajamas, wearing
a hat.

OWEN

Hey!

SYLVIA

What, what are you doing up? It's nowhere
near lunchtime.

OWEN

I know that.

SYLVIA

(*Noticing him*) What's—wrong?

OWEN

I don't know. Nothing. Everything.

SYLVIA

What exactly are you accusing me of?

OWEN

What?

SYLVIA

Why are you—?

OWEN

Accusing you?

SYLVIA

Where did you find that hat?

OWEN

Hey. I can be as mental as the next guy.
(*Approaching her*)

SYLVIA

Don't smile. You look depraved.

OWEN

>Do you know what equidistance is, Sylvia?
>Don't—go. Listen. Just—would you—

SYLVIA

>Is this another geometry lesson?

OWEN

>No, this isn't a geometry lesson. I'm talking
>about us for a change. Separated by equal
>distances; you and me.

SYLVIA

>This is getting cold.

OWEN

>You thought we didn't have anything in
>common, well, you're wrong. We are the only
>two people in the world who know exactly
>how far apart from each other we are,
>because the farther I get from you, the
>farther you get from—I had this all worked
>out. I know, I know what this distance is. I—I
>know. I can get closer. I can—get—closer.
>And then you can—you can—see?

SYLVIA

>What are you talking about?

OWEN

>—get closer, and—

SYLVIA

>Owen.

OWEN

>We can be close. Again. See? We just need to
>do things together. We need to get away from
>here and—do things. Let's go to Paris for
>God's sake. What are we waiting for? You've

been wanting to leave. We could—both leave
together.

SYLVIA

I think you're missing the point.

OWEN

Am I? Not really. Not when you think about it.
And I've been thinking about it a lot. I have.
All morning. And last night. When you didn't
bother coming to bed. But, hey.

Beat.

See? I'm not a square, Sylvia. You wanted to
stay up and talk to Mr. Lawrence. That's—
that's—

SYLVIA

Actually—

OWEN

I—understand. I get it. He fascinates you.
Because he's—well I'm not sure what he is—
spontaneous. But there's still something,
Sylvia. When you came into the room last
night, I was still awake. I could feel you sitting
there, on the edge of the bed, just looking at
me; mulling the whole thing over in your
mind. You haven't decided. See? And that's—
that's—encouraging, I think. You haven't
given up. You just need me to come a little
distance. I'll come a long distance.

SYLVIA

I'll go make another cup.

OWEN

Sylvia, it's not me you need to run away from.
It's this house. Forget the damn coffee. This

Boarding house = fish bowl.

87

house is destroying our relationship.
Everything. It's been too easy for us to make
absolutely nothing of ourselves here.

SYLVIA

It hasn't been easy at all. It's actually been
quite a lot of work.

OWEN

I mean, look what happened to Lobachevsky.

SYLVIA

Who?

OWEN

Sylvia. Please. The founder of post-Euclidean
geometry. It wasn't until he left his hometown
that he finally got some perspective.

She thinks she smells something.

OWEN

It opened his mind, Sylvia.

SYLVIA

Wherever you go, Owen, you take yourself
with you.

OWEN

(*Beat*) No you don't. Where'd you get that?
Out of a fortune cookie?

SYLVIA

Waldo Emerson. If you must know.

OWEN

Really?

SYLVIA

Someone.

OWEN

    Paris will change me, Sylvia.

SYLVIA

    I just—

    IRIS enters surreptitiously.

OWEN

    There are certain parts of that city that were
    designed according to very strict
    mathematical principles. Arcane principles,
    but principles nevertheless. This place has no
    principles, Sylvia. That's the whole problem.
    Just mountains and a bunch of water. You
    never know where you are here.

SYLVIA

    You know exactly where you are.

OWEN

    And that's the whole problem.

    Beat.

SYLVIA

    You don't even speak French.

OWEN

    French?

SYLVIA

    Just one thing worries me. Just—What
    happens after you've got your little Parisian
    cold water flat?

OWEN

    Who said anything about cold water? Don't
    they have hot water in France?

SYLVIA

After you've sat in there all day, day after day,
doing what you do here. What will your
dream be, then? At least here you have one.

OWEN

I could—I could do something with my
drawings. Look. Can you get more abstract?

SYLVIA

Is that the toast?

OWEN

Last night, Sylvia. Just—Sylvia.

SYLVIA

I didn't come into the room last night.

OWEN

Then, who did?

MR. LAWRENCE enters.

LAWRENCE

I had a little situation with that toaster in
there.

They all look at one another.

SYLVIA

I thought something was burning.

SYLVIA exits to the kitchen.

OWEN

So.

LAWRENCE

So. Yeah. So.

OWEN

So. What happened at the cannery?

LAWRENCE
    When?

OWEN
    You were going to go down this morning to
    apply for a job, I thought.

LAWRENCE
    Should I?

OWEN
    Well, I don't know. That was the plan. Wasn't
    that the plan?

LAWRENCE
    Right.

OWEN
    You don't know what I'm talking about, do
    you?

LAWRENCE
    I know what you're talking about. The plan.

OWEN
    Mr. Lawrence. I, uh, called the Provincial
    Hospital this morning.

LAWRENCE
    Oh. O.K.

OWEN
    To inquire if there were any missing—

LAWRENCE
    Sure.

OWEN
    With all these air raid drills, you never know
    who might have walked away from where.

LAWRENCE
    You think, maybe, Miss Rose—?

OWEN
What?

LAWRENCE
What?

OWEN
I was talking about you.

LAWRENCE
Oh, sure.

Beat.

Could you repeat that?

OWEN
As it turns out, all inmates are accounted for.

LAWRENCE
That's—Yeah?

OWEN
But I asked if they might come down here
and have a chat with you anyway. I hope you
don't mind.

Door bell.

Oh. Maybe that's them.

IRIS quickly steps in.

IRIS
I'll go.

SYLVIA enters.

If it's people from an asylum, you might not
want to answer the door in pajamas and a
pork pie hat.

SYLVIA
Asylum?

OWEN
What?

LAWRENCE
What—what's happening?

SYLVIA
That's what I'd like to know.

Doorbell.

OWEN
I'll get it.

IRIS
No, I'll get it.

SYLVIA
I'll—get it.

SYLVIA goes to answer the door.

IRIS
(*to Lawrence*) Act sane.

He does.

IRIS
On second thought, go hide under my bed.

LAWRENCE exits.

SYLVIA comes back.

OWEN
Who—who was it?

SYLVIA
Fuller Brush.

OWEN
That guy is—taunting us. What?

SYLVIA

> Asylum, Owen? What if he is crazy? Why
> would you ever want to subject him to that
> kind of institutionalization?

IRIS

> (*Trying the word in her mouth*)
> Institutionalization.

OWEN

> I didn't call anyone. I didn't—call anyone;
> alright? I was just trying to scare the guy a
> little. Bring him to his—I was going to say
> senses. Don't look at me like that. I'm just
> trying to protect this family, Sylvia.

SYLVIA

> From what?

OWEN

> From—from what? We don't know anything
> about this man. What do we know about him?
> Except that he makes bubbles with his saliva.

SYLVIA

> What do we need to know about him? Is it
> really necessary to become intimate with the
> guests?

OWEN

> You tell me.

SYLVIA

> What does that mean?

OWEN

> You were the one who was in his—room last
> night.

> *SYLVIA looks at IRIS.*

IRIS

He forced it out of me. Look: snake bite.

SYLVIA

Go somewhere.

IRIS

Where?

SYLVIA exits.

SYLVIA

Anywhere. All of you. Go.

IRIS

What did I do?

OWEN

You heard her.

IRIS

You owe me a dollar, by the way.

OWEN

Whatever happened to school? Don't you go to school anymore?

IRIS

I'd rather not spend the last few hours of my childhood making a diorama for a squirrel, thanks.

OWEN

My wife doesn't love me.

He removes his hat.

IRIS

I do.

As OWEN wanders off, she calls to him

IRIS

There's still hope.

An air raid siren.

IRIS crawls under the drafting table. The siren ends. SYLVIA enters. Looks about.

No one. She sighs. Covers her face with her hands. MR. LAWRENCE rushes in.

LAWRENCE

What was that?

SYLVIA

It's just a drill.

LAWRENCE

Maybe I should—get out of here.

SYLVIA

What? No. No, Mr. Lawrence. My husband is an idiot. He's—

LAWRENCE

I don't—think I should, uh, I should go.

SYLVIA

Well, if you, fine, if you think you should—if you—really—if you—

LAWRENCE

Or—

SYLVIA

No. Stay. Well—go if you like.

LAWRENCE

I don't—know—what I should do. Should I—what?

SYLVIA

Don't go. Mr. Lawrence, I want you to stay. I don't want you to stay but I—certainly would like you to—stay. I—We all—. All of us—

LAWRENCE
    Miss Rose?

SYLVIA
    Well, she's—

LAWRENCE
    And your husband.

SYLVIA
    He's just a little on edge because our
    marriage is—. We don't usually threaten to
    have the guests committed.

LAWRENCE
    I don't want to hurt him.

SYLVIA
    Of course not. Of course—not. You're too
    kind for that. You're too thoughtful and too
    kind.

        A beat. She kisses him. Another beat.

    Mr. Lawrence. What's happening?

LAWRENCE
    Where?

SYLVIA
    Listen to me; I have something to say. I just—
    have to—think what it is for a minute. I—

        Beat.

    God, when you look at me like that I can't—
    I—please, don't just stand there. Don't—

        He goes.

SYLVIA
    Wait. Where are you—?

LAWRENCE
    What?

SYLVIA
    Mr. Lawrence—

LAWRENCE
    I'm confused.

SYLVIA
    You're confused! What was I thinking? Last
    night—last night was—Going into your room
    without knocking. I'm a Catholic, Mr.
    Lawrence. Mind you, the whole world—every
    time you turn on the damn radio. It's no
    excuse, but we just seem to be destroying
    ourselves. That's the—terrible—that's the—
    what's happening to the Latin Mass? What am
    I saying? I'm saying that—what I'm saying is
    that one day, one day a woman finds herself
    sitting across the room from this—man she
    married and thinking, "Wait a minute, what
    am I doing here?" I don't love you, Mr.
    Lawrence; it was a notion—some—When I
    think of you standing there, last night, with
    that look of—oh, Mr. Lawrence; trying to
    hide yourself with that fuzzy little souvenir
    Eskimo—thing. What must you think of me? I
    just—I don't—love you. I only wanted you. Do
    you understand? The way I've never, ever
    wanted—

    Turning, she sees OWEN. Beat.

    Owen.

98

OWEN

Have you seen the rope I tried to hang myself
with last year?

SYLVIA

Owen—

OWEN

Don't let me interrupt this.

LAWRENCE

And hey—I'm not—crazy, okay? This is not
my—mind!

OWEN

Oh, it isn't.

SYLVIA

Excuse me. I have to—to ——out of the
freezer.

SYLVIA runs off.

LAWRENCE

And another thing. Another thing.

OWEN stops; turns.

OWEN

What?

LAWRENCE

What?

OWEN

Mr. Lawrence. Mr. Lawrence—I don't mean
to pry into your private life, but. Did you
have—let's just come right out and say it—
(*intimate*) relations with my wife last night?

LAWRENCE

Inti—what?

OWEN

 (Intimate) *Intimate!*

LAWRENCE

 What? Oh.

OWEN

 Uh huh? Uh huh?

LAWRENCE

 Well I think there was some kind of—
 miscommunication there, sir.

OWEN

 Misc—? I haven't had—those kind of
 relations with my wife for about two years.
 That's miscommunication. You were dancing
 around your room, for her, last night with an
 Ookpik, apparently. That's—communication.
 That's—

LAWRENCE

 We didn't, sort of, do anything—much.

OWEN

 Did you sort of do anything—at all?

LAWRENCE

 She took off some of her things, I think.

OWEN

 Things. Uh, huh. By "things," Mr. Lawrence,
 do you mean, shoes and things, or—or
 brassieres and things?

LAWRENCE

 I don't—I don't remember?

OWEN

 You don't remember. And then?

LAWRENCE
And then she sat down on the bed.

OWEN
Uh, huh. Uh, huh.

LAWRENCE
And then she, yes, and then she cried.

OWEN
She cried?

LAWRENCE
And then she fell asleep.

OWEN
Really?

LAWRENCE
Yeah. And that's when I came into your room.

Beat.

OWEN
That was you?

LAWRENCE
Sorry. I shouldn't have done that. That was an unusual thing.

OWEN
It, yes—it was.

LAWRENCE
Apologies, sir.

OWEN
You—you—

LAWRENCE
I just wanted to—— absorb, perhaps, a little of your beautiful despair.

OWEN

Well. I don't appreciate my despair being
absorbed, Mr. Lawrence. Despair? People
don't just waltz into other people's rooms in
the middle of the night and—and—and look
at them.

LAWRENCE

I just wanted to be part of this. You know?
They made me think things and see things—

OWEN

Who did?

LAWRENCE

I don't—know. I just want to be part of this
instead of—I just want to be part of it.

OWEN

Well, I don't want you to be part of it. Part of,
part of what?

LAWRENCE

The geometry.

OWEN

Uh, huh. I'm a simple man, Mr. Lawrence.
Well, alright, not a simple man. A man of few
words. O.K., that's not strictly true. A man
without artifice. Alright, a man of the
moment. Let's see. A man—a man—I'm a
man, Mr. Lawrence. I think we can reliably say
that I'm a man. Let's just leave it at that.

LAWRENCE

Sure.

OWEN

Geometry?

Beat.

LAWRENCE

Yeah. Or—yeah.

Lights change. LAWRENCE runs off.

IRIS

A math question. If Mr. Lawrence likes my father, and my father likes my mother, and my mother likes Mr. Lawrence, then approximately what time will Miss Rose arrive home from work? Answer—

MISS ROSE enters. She sits, lighting a cigarette. IRIS pops up, giving her a start.

ROSE

What are you doing under there?

IRIS

Trying to learn all I can about being an adult before I actually become one.

Would you like an aspirin for that hangover, Miss Rose?

ROSE

Guess what I did today, dearie?

IRIS

Does it have anything to do with evisceration?

ROSE

I called the R.C.M.P.; about our secretive guest.

Beat.

IRIS

No you didn't.

ROSE

> There's already one spy in this house too many.

IRIS

> They probably just thought you were a crank. Like when you complained about that peeping tom on the corner, in the red hat, who turned out to be a stop sign.

ROSE

> They pressed me for details.

IRIS

> You mean like what Mr. Lawrence looks like with his pants down?

ROSE

> How about that aspirin? And be quick about it.

> *IRIS finds the aspirin, then pockets them.*

IRIS

> I'll see what I can find.

> *She starts off quickly, as SYLVIA enters.*

SYLVIA

> What are you up to?

IRIS

> Nothing.

SYLVIA

> (*seeing MISS ROSE*) Miss Rose. Legion not open yet?

ROSE

> How's the wrist?

OWEN

> (*From off*) Sylvia!

SYLVIA

    Excuse me.

SYLVIA exits into the kitchen. OWEN enters.

OWEN

    Sylvia? (*Stopping*) Miss—Rose.

ROSE

    Do you have to be so formal with me all the time?

OWEN

    Have you—uh—seen my wife?

ROSE

    Things are going better for the two of you I hope.

OWEN

    Why wouldn't they be?

ROSE

    She's a little unpredictable these days, poor thing. One minute she's tumbling over a suitcase to get out of here, and the next thing you know, she's up and about, all smiles and what have you. Where's the new boarder?

OWEN

    I—don't—

ROSE

    I sure hope things work out between you and Sylvia. It would be a shame for her to—you know.

OWEN

    It—it—would.

ROSE

This great big house, and no one to look after you. Poor, sweet Owen.

Beat.

If anybody needs me, I'll be upstairs, soaking in a nice sudsy lavender bath.

Exits. On her way, running into IRIS; a little out of breath with a glass of water and some crushed pills.

IRIS

Miss Rose. Your aspirins. I took the liberty of mooshing them up for you.

ROSE

(*Too hung over to care*) Thanks, honey.

She takes the pills and water, as OWEN goes into the kitchen.

IRIS

You're welcome.

MISS ROSE exits. IRIS comes downstage, capping her father's prescription.

IRIS

If she really did call the R.C.M.P, and they happen to show up, it's best, I think, to keep her out of the picture.

LAWRENCE
R.C.M.P.?

IRIS

You haven't done anything wrong.

LAWRENCE
You, you promised.

IRIS

It wasn't me.

LAWRENCE

Now I have to leave here.

IRIS

Why? No. Why?

LAWRENCE

I can't trust anybody here.

IRIS

This is where you belong.

LAWRENCE

I don't. I don't—belong. I have anti-social
tendencies. O.K.?

IRIS

Have you forgotten what you really came back
for, Mr. Lawrence?

Beat.

How many times do I have to explain?

LAWRENCE

How about one more time?

IRIS

If you leave so does my mother. If she leaves,
so does my father. It isn't an orphanage I'm
so worried about. Miss Rose is my godmother.
That makes her my legal guardian, for your
information. I've been through all of my
parent's papers. It's right down there in black
and white. You can't—you can't—you—you—
(*quietly*) can't.

You're holding all this together.

LAWRENCE

Well, I can't do that. I can't hold it together. I can't hold myself together. I don't need that kind of responsibility. So don't—so don't—

Beat.

Listen to me. I was a little girl, too, once or; no. A little boy—once. I was—I was—Grown ups can be very disappointing, Iris, because of their size—or. You look up to them, is why; but it's only their size. That's the only—you see? If—if grown ups were smaller, then—then—I mean if they were tiny, then—like that size, say—you wouldn't look up to them so much. Does that—make sense?

IRIS

No.

She falls into his lap.

IRIS

Mr. Lawrence.

LAWRENCE

I'm not all I'm cracked up to be.

IRIS

It's all so paradoxical.

LAWRENCE

I did something, once. I don't remember what it was, but it was—not good.

IRIS

How do you know, if you don't remember?

LAWRENCE

Because they want to get inside my head, and—get it—out.

IRIS

    Who?

LAWRENCE

    I don't know. I have to get out here, just for a
    while. O.K? I—I need you to help me.

IRIS

    I would do anything for you. But you can't
    leave. Promise and hope to die.

LAWRENCE

    I just need to hide out for a little bit.

IRIS

    And then you'll come back?

    Beat.

LAWRENCE

    You don't know very much about me.

IRIS

    But I do. I—do. I've known you since grade
    three.

    Holding him.

    Sometimes, when you were there in your little
    bowl, I used to close my eyes and pretend that
    we were swimming together. Swimming
    together in circles. Remember?

    Pause.

LAWRENCE

    —Yeah …

IRIS

    Even now, your skin is nothing like human
    skin. It's golden, see; shimmering. Look. And
    your eyes so black and round. I understand

you. You're just not very good at being human. But Mr. Lawrence, nobody is.

They look at one another, sadly.

IRIS

I know a place where you can hide. It's under the cannery. In the pilings, there's a broken up old boat. I'll show you.

LAWRENCE

I—need to make myself look different.

IRIS

Less inscrutable?

LAWRENCE

Something.

IRIS

Miss Rose has some Lady Clairol red hair dye. It doesn't work for her, but it might just work for you.

SYLVIA enters from the kitchen.

IRIS

Hello, mother.

SYLVIA

What are you up to?

IRIS

Nothing.

SYLVIA

What's she up to?

LAWRENCE

Nothing.

IRIS

Excuse me.

She runs off.

SYLVIA

She only acts good when she's up to
something bad.

LAWRENCE

Yeah.

Beat.

I've decided, ma'am. I'm—gonna get going,
now.

A pause. SYLVIA sits.

SYLVIA

I guess I sort of—I guess I knew that.

LAWRENCE

You're a very nice woman. You have—nice
hair, and—

SYLVIA

Thank you.

LAWRENCE

Your husband is a very good man.

SYLVIA

He is; yes.

LAWRENCE

I don't think you should leave him.

*Unseen, OWEN opens the kitchen door, then
quietly, slowly closes it again.*

SYLVIA

Sure. Why not stay? Inhabit this space here
like a—ball of dust. I just thought for a
moment—well, what difference does it make,
what I thought? I don't even have the will to

111

leave anymore. But I don't have the desire to stay. It's—I don't suppose you could use some company. On your—no. No, that would be— no.

LAWRENCE

I don't—

SYLVIA

Don't—say it. I apologize for last night, Mr. Lawrence. Could we just forget about that? I'll go with you as far as the bus stop, and then we can—take different buses or something. Have you ever been to Australia?

LAWRENCE

He loves you very much.

SYLVIA

Mr. Lawrence. For twelve years, now, I've thought, well, it's enough to be loved. But you have to love back. You have to love back.

A beat. She goes. OWEN enters from the kitchen.

LAWRENCE

Sir.

OWEN

What are you doing?

LAWRENCE

Sir?

OWEN

You can't just walk out on my wife like this.

LAWRENCE

Sir. The thing is. I might be in a little bit of trouble.

OWEN

Never mind that. I want you to stay. I don't want you to stay. But I am asking you to. Alright, I'm begging you. Please. This is humiliating. Mr. Lawrence. I've suddenly, cogently, had an idea. You want to be part of the geometry? Fine. You know what a triangle is.

Beat, as LAWRENCE thinks.

OWEN

It's a three-sided figure, Mr. Lawrence; take my word for it. You can stay and be her lover, is what I'm—If that's what she wants. If that's what she—I don't know what she wants. Who knows what she wants? But I won't stand in the way. I won't. I can't. You can even— absorb my despair, or whatever it is you— spontaneously—I don't care. I don't— Anything. As long as Sylvia doesn't—go. I know it's insane. It's insane. It's completely and absolutely—it's. Thank you for bringing insanity into our, thank you, into our lives. Don't just stand there, watching me humiliate myself; please. I love her. I can't let her go. Without her, I'm nothing. Actually, with her I'm nothing, but without her I'm not even— I'm—Mr. Lawrence. Mr. Lawrence, please.

Beat.

What sort of trouble?

MISS ROSE enters, hair in a towel; drugged up.

ROSE

Am I interrupting—something?

OWEN

No. Yes.

LAWRENCE

(*On leaving*) Excuse me, ma'am.

ROSE

Don't run away on my account.

OWEN

Mr. Lawrence.

LAWRENCE goes. OWEN sits, ruined.

ROSE

My goodness. All this running around.
Upstairs, and downstairs. People packing
suitcases. A hot bath is what you all need. My
lips feel—Owen, you look so glum. Don't look
so glum. I hope I haven't been the cause of
anything. Have I been the cause? Shame on
me. Shame, shame on me. Not minding my
own business. Forgive me. I'm sorry, Owen. I
don't know what for, why should I be sorry?
I'm sorry.

OWEN

It doesn't matter.

ROSE

Of course it does. No; you're right. It doesn't.
I'm not sorry. Oh, but I am. For you. I'm
sorry for you. Poor Owen. Your wife up in her
room, packing her bag. And you loved her so
much. And she didn't love you.

Beat.

It's time you were loved, Owen. You deserve
to be loved. Look at me.

OWEN

    I thought I could, maybe, change her by attrition.

ROSE

    Sure, hon.

       Beat.

    What's that?

OWEN

    Like the way water eventually carves those odd shapes into rocks. Of course, that—takes about a trillion years.

ROSE

    Does it? Does it?

       She stumbles a bit.

OWEN

    Are you—?

ROSE

    It's terrible, you know, when a marriage falls apart. I mean if two people can't even work things out—well, for goodness sake—what hope is there for this sad old world? Oh, my robe. It's got a—mind of it's own.

       Coming close to him, sloppily.

    I'm sure that's why I've never married. Or maybe it's because the right person never—ever—came along.

OWEN

    What difference would it make if they did?

ROSE

    You tell me.

OWEN

    People are straight lines.

ROSE

    But tell me about this interesting
    phenomenon where they join up again.

OWEN

    What in God's name is that scent, Miss Rose?

      He coughs.

ROSE

    Lavender, hon. Your favorite.

OWEN

    Who told you that?

      A beat. Barely able to stay awake, MISS ROSE
      falls towards Owen.

ROSE

    My goodness. Those—aspirin.

      She leans, mouth drooping, as OWEN tries to
      extricate himself. Free of MISS ROSE, he exits. A
      gasp echoes through the house. Music.

      IRIS appears; shaken.

IRIS

    Will wonders never cease?

      She descends the stairs in a trance. Reaching
      bottom, water drips from above.

Mr. Lawrence, running into the bathroom to
change the color of his hair, seems to have
slipped on the wet tiles, falling, smashing his
head against the wall or the sink, and
tumbling backwards into Miss Rose's scummy
bath. I think he's drowned by the looks of

him. It's like he took this one big breath and
he's just—holding it, underwater.

> *Beat.*

The smell of lavender is quite—
overwhelming. Sweat drips down the
windows. Down the porcelain. Lady Clairol
hair dye is splooshed everywhere. It looks
fantastically like blood. If I didn't know better,
I'd say it was a murder scene. He's just sort of
floating sideways in the tub, looking a little
like—well—a little like a dead fish.

SYLVIA

What?

> *Beat.*

You're joking. Are you joking? You're joking.

IRIS

Think someone might have pushed him?

SYLVIA

Where's your—father?

> *SYLVIA disappears. Music. IRIS kneels.*

IRIS

I've never seen a dead person before. Except
for my grandmother, but that doesn't count,
because that's the way she already looked.

> *SYLVIA appears from around the corner. A*
> *beat.*

SYLVIA

Go and get some blankets. Hurry.

IRIS

It might have been an accident, you know.

SYLVIA

A what? I'll run around and get the car.

IRIS

What car? We sold it. Remember?

SYLVIA

We did?

IRIS

I'll get the Dominion shopping cart.

*SYLVIA exits for a beat. SYLVIA drags MR.
LAWRENCE, noisily, down the stairs.*

IRIS

I think my mother suddenly believes that my
father is capable of murder. Which is sort of
lovely in a way. It means she thinks he's
capable of something.

*SYLVIA drags MR. LAWRENCE across the room
to the kitchen.*

SYLVIA

Give me a hand. No. What am I thinking?
Forget the damned car.

IRIS

You said damn.

SYLVIA

Forget the car.

IRIS

We don't have a car.

SYLVIA

We'll take him down to the—what?—to the
water. What's wrong? What are you doing?

IRIS

My nose is bleeding.

SYLVIA

No it isn't. Get some Kleenex. What am I
doing?

*IRIS runs out. SYLVIA props up MR.
LAWRENCE. MISS ROSE wakes. Seeing them. A
beat.*

ROSE

Look at me. I'm on my way up in the world.

She passes them.

*MISS ROSE stumbles up the stairs. Then
SYLVIA and IRIS drag the body off, through the
kitchen.*

*A knock at the door. Another knock. OWEN
appears from the cellar.*

OWEN

Why doesn't somebody answer the door?

*Another knock. Goes to answer the door. Lights
change.*

IRIS

(*Appearing, mopping up the floor*) Two men in
raincoats appear. But they don't stay long.
Our inscrutable guest is nowhere to be found.
A trail of smelly bathwater, but nothing more.

OWEN

Goodnight Gentlemen. Goodnight.

Doors closes. Lights change.

OWEN

Where's your mother?

IRIS

Dealing with the body.

OWEN

    Oh.

       Wanders off. Stops.

    Body?

       Music. Lights change and IRIS is alone.

IRIS

    As my father and I hurry and make our way
    down to the water, a car passes. It could be
    me for all you know, years from now,
    revisiting the scene of these adventures and
    these little crimes.

    The water is very still tonight. But the boats
    are grinding against their moorings, like the
    sound of something tearing itself wide open.

SYLVIA

    Well, if it was an accident, then we'll just have
    to take him and put him back in the tub.

IRIS

    It'll look unnatural.

OWEN

    She's right.

       They study the body for a moment.

OWEN

    You actually thought I—killed him?

SYLVIA

    Not intentionally.

OWEN

    I could have.

SYLVIA

    Really?

IRIS

I don't think we have a choice here.

OWEN

If this is where he came from, then this is where we leave him.

Light change.

IRIS

We give Mr. Lawrence a little push off the end of the pier.

Splash.

As he sinks, my parents turn quickly away, but I watch for a moment; say another prayer for his little soul. Then he pops back up to the surface. And floats along the pilings.

They call her away.

OWEN

Iris!

SYLVIA

Please!

IRIS

What'll happen to the world now, I cannot say?

SYLVIA

Iris!

IRIS

We make our way back along the street, now, under the dull buzzing of the lamplights. The fog has lifted a little and the sky is cast in an eerie white fluorescence. My father takes my hand in his. Then he looks at my mother

starts to laugh. She's so surprised that she
starts to laugh along with him.

SYLVIA and OWEN start to laugh.

Suddenly she grabs my other hand and we
start running now. We're running together as
fast as we can. Like three best friends out on a
crazy Halloween prank. They're both holding
my hands. I can't believe this moment is happening. And then—and then they lift me up.
Up, up in the air. Oh, God.

She holds herself suspended for a moment.

At this moment, I wouldn't trade places with
Princess Anne for anything.

*Lights up, as they fall about, breathless,
laughing.*

SYLVIA

What are we doing? Oh, my God.

Suddenly serious.

What have we, what have we done?

OWEN

Iris. Get away from the window.

SYLVIA

Have we gone completely, stark-raving—?

OWEN

Yes. Yes, we have. We have.

SYLVIA

Oh. (*Seriously*) Poor Mr. Lawrence.

OWEN

Poor Mr. Lawrence.

122

IRIS

Poor Mr. Lawrence.

SYLVIA and OWEN look at each other for a long moment. They caress. They kiss. IRIS, watching them, wipes a tear from her eye. Beside a record player, now, she plays them a song. SYLVIA and OWEN waltz, looking over each other's shoulder. IRIS, off to the side, picks up her empty goldfish bowl, and watches them through it. They stop.

SYLVIA

Look, Owen. There's a girl in the goldfish bowl.

Mood → *The lights change. SYLVIA goes off and OWEN follows. IRIS looks about the whole room. Stops.*

IRIS

I will hold onto this night forever; this sadness and this happiness all at once. Goodbye—Mr. Lawrence.

→ *Pause, as she caresses the bowl. Lights change.*

Well, before you know it, it's morning on our street. The sun isn't shining, but at least it's trying to.

MISS ROSE enters, dropping a paper on the table.

MISS ROSE

The Russians are backing down.

IRIS

Disappointed?

123

MISS ROSE
>Oh. And some man was found washed up on the beach last night.

IRIS
>Will wonders never cease?

MISS ROSE
>Where's Mr. Lawrence?

IRIS
>It's all a complete mystery.

MISS ROSE
>Nothing's a mystery for long.

>>*Beat. MISS ROSE exits. IRIS studies the paper.*

IRIS
>I'm the only one, of course, who knows Mr. Lawrence's true identity. And his purpose in coming.

>>*OWEN enters from the kitchen with breakfast things.*

OWEN
>Bonjour!

IRIS
>I think this might be the end of an era. Or maybe it's the beginning of one.

OWEN
>I think you might be right.

IRIS
>I'm really feeling rather blithesome, this morning.

OWEN
>What would you think if we went to Paris this year, Iris?

IRIS

Who would look after me?

OWEN

We'll all go.

IRIS

That would be—sublime.

OWEN

It would.

IRIS

Can you flip that spatula in the air, and catch
it with one hand?

He does so.

That proves it. I'm not even squinting my eyes
and I can see that you're happy.

OWEN

Who? Me?

*OWEN, almost unable to contain his happiness,
returns to the kitchen.*

OWEN

(*Calling from off*) Sylvia! Breakfast is ready.

IRIS

(*Casually perusing the paper*) You know, I was
thinking how I'd be much better off with a
budgie this time. If I could get it to talk,
imagine; it could go to confession for me. Or,
who knows; maybe I'll just get some friends.
Then again, we could always get a television.
Sister Anamelda says they're the devil's
instrument. I think that's recommendation
enough, don't you?

IRIS suddenly notices her mother at the top of the stairs, with a suitcase, and gasps, without a sound. IRIS tries to speak. SYLVIA puts a finger to her lips, smiles. IRIS watches helplessly, as SYLVIA descends.

OWEN

(*From the kitchen*) Did you know that if you stand under the Arc de Triomphe, Iris—you can see all the way to the Louvre. And if you look the other way, practically the same distance in the other direction. It's the intersection of twelve streets, you know. And honest to God, Iris. When you stand there, you'd swear you were at the centre of the whole world.

With another sad little smile, SYLVIA disappears. A moment. IRIS, as she speaks, begins her transformation into an adult, putting on a raincoat, undoing her hair.

IRIS

If only I could open my mouth and make a sound that would reach back through those years, mother. As you unlatch the door, and that sudden breeze rushes in. As down our street bits of leaves and paper blow about, and you hurry quickly, quietly away. This is the moment when I know for certain that there is nothing, past or present, that could ever make things other than they are. That chance, alone, makes them that way.

OWEN enters from the kitchen, but now he is distant, in the past.

OWEN

    Iris?

IRIS

    This, I remember, is when it happens, father.

OWEN

    What is it?

IRIS

    The last moment of my childhood.

      Beat. OWEN, noticing the front door is open,
      goes up the stairs, as IRIS sits with her goldfish
      bowl, remembering. As the lights fade, a melody.

      Blackout.

      The End.

(best)

theist
Least believable character
Strongest character
Weakest
Least/most Likable
True

Themes • childhood/adult transition
        • insanity, altered states of mind
        • Religion

Dominant theme ?

• Material culture
• Authority figures   dysfunction
    • parents — m
    • RCMP
    • Dag H.
    • Nuns
    • Religion / Re Budhist
    • Br. Rosal1h
    • Bonjour